This Book Belongs To

Printed in Great Britain
by Amazon

65322996R00066